Caffeine and Nicotine
-By Hannah Farmer

ISBN: 9781720080763

Dedication

For all of the amazing people in my life who push me when I need direction. I am forever grateful for your attempts at keeping me sane and out of my own head. You mean more to me than you will ever know.

Petunias

I stay, but oh God do I wish to run
Run far away and never return
To a place that knows nothing of my existence so I can garden in the
afternoon

Bothered by no one asking menial questions as I sweat trying to plant
petunias in the summer sun
No one will ask for a cup of sugar, or to borrow my lawnmower
No one will pretend to like me over tea as we discuss neighborhood gossip
Telling me who paid for plastic surgery, becoming fake like their care for me

I stay, but oh God do I wish to run
Run far away and never return
To a place that knows nothing of my existence so I can garden in the
afternoon

Enjoying the silence around me, no voices lilted in a way that makes me
want to vomit
No one to stand over me oblivious to the fact they are blocking the warmth
of the sun on my face

No one expecting me to share feelings with them when I don't have any
Telling me to be less prickly, maybe I am unapproachable because I don't
want to be approached

I stay, but oh God do I wish to run
Run far away and never return
To a place that knows nothing of my existence so I can garden in the
afternoon

Toska

My heart beats against the cage you put around it
Thumping so violent my ears ring with the noise
Useful in biology and wasted in emotion
I am a shell

Adjectives

In the scents carried on the breeze, I discovered
In the branches that grab me, I searched
Sunset and sunrise, day to night I wandered

In the green of the grass, I explored
In the blue of the sky, I searched
High and low, left to right I wandered

In the warmth of the sunshine on my face, I searched
In the moonlight whispers through the trees, I listened
Growing upward and tumbling down, I wandered

In the melodies of babies, I searched
In the soul of another's eyes, I examined
Life to death, I wandered

In my wasted life, I scrutinized
In my last words, I searched
Across the river Jordan, I wander

Mother

My stomach drops as I free fall

I can feel the phases of the moon caressing my back one by one as I
descend towards the inevitable
Greenery getting closer, flourishing as they stand, hundreds of mouths
gaping ready to receive flesh
A flower blooms on my fingertips as I plunge deeper towards the savage
dwelling

I never dreamed of smelling like the earth more than I did at that moment
The scent of petrichor and dirt
I wanted to smell the rain so greatly that I tasted it
I gnawed hungry at the green grass and the topsoil; I consumed the proud
cedar forests and tree bark
Oh to feel the essence of fresh tobacco fields and cactus blossoms waft
from my palms

To carry the breath of nature on my skin
To envelop those around me in the thick aroma of the earth's crust warmed
by the shining sun
Clay-rich and red, soft and calling I hear my name
Birds float past me and I close my eyes

A welcome sacrifice to the mother I will be

The Count

We count from birth
Counting 1, 2, 3
Counting bottles, counting diapers, counting toys

Counting, counting, counting 2, 3, 4
Counting cars, counting friends, counting even more
Counting, counting, counting 3, 4, 5

Counting work, counting possessions, counting lives
Counting, counting, counting 5, 4, 3, 2

Then we arrive at the end
Learning all our time was spent

Counting, counting, counting, 3, 2, 1

Deadly VI

Pampered and deserving, spoiled like thick yellow milk
Can't you see? Your frog has been a prince all along

Coveting the shiny, discarding the unpolished
Only the most expensive oils will coat his skin

I light the match and ignite the fire
All that will be left is jewel and bone

Purity

Today I thought the snow glorious
Paying no mind to the cold
But instead laughing at the brilliance that is this world

Today I thought the snow glorious
As if these tiny specks of white had come down from above to cleanse the
hatred
To shed light into the darkest part of my soul
To overcome the rage and war that is this planet and in its place instill joy
and peace

Today I thought the snow glorious
As it billowed down from the heavens
Oh, the path one single flake must have followed!
Like tiny bits of our souls given up throughout the years
Returning to us in crystallized magnificence

As I sit here and ponder on it
Put in a state of utter wonderment
Baffled by its profound beauty and effect on our troubled planet
I am a child again

Nothing I have ever done has mattered before this moment
I am new and I am pure
My heart soars and my spirit lifts upwards as I shed a tear
For today, I thought the snow glorious indeed

Nodus Tollens

My love, I fear we haven't much time
It's coming for me in the darkness
Inching closer, closer, closer

I hear it hiss, feel it clawing at me
Please don't let it take me my darling
Why aren't you helping me?

It has a hold of me now and I understand
My dearest boy you never existed in my world
In between obscurity and madness

It is all consuming
Holding power over me
As I lay on the floor speaking these words to you

I know the darkness has lived in me all along

Watchman

As I stand solid, tall, and dignified
I watch you pass
Going about day by day, never noticing me, but still, I watch

I have seen your pain and joy
Witnessed your hopes and fears
I watch your obstacles and turmoil

I celebrate as you finally notice me
Rejoicing in your happiness
I tremble as you cut me, hacking away bit by bit

Always silent, but always watching
I see you come to me for warmth in times of bitter cold
Providing refuge the best I can, and still, you continue to cut away

As you use me to sustain life I am ever so silent, but watching
Where I once was solid, tall, and dignified
You've torn me down

Even though I no longer stand, my roots ripped bloody from the ground
I still rejoice in your triumphs and shed a tear for your tragedies
Still, just as silent, I watch

Matter

Too bad when it mattered we didn't matter enough,
What's the matter with you?
Wishing completely love would matter when nothing mattered most

You made me feel as though I didn't matter
To not only you but to the world, to anything that might matter
What matters?

Not the matter you are made of, but the substance that matter can hold
However, if the matter doesn't matter
What you mold yourself into must matter

Make yourself matter in a world where the wrong things matter and the
things that should have mattered never did
A great deal of work was done on this matter, that matter is you
You, who must matter the most

Deadly V

Tremble before me and feel my fury
A grizzly caught in your trap

Thrashing about hoping to be unleashed
Red blood makes a puddle as it drip, drip, drips

Cutting, eroding piece by piece until there is no more
You will never be whole again

The Tree

Waiting for rebirth
Broken, twisted I am cold
Spring breathes me to life

Emotions Downloading

Satire, humor
This is funny
Laugh- ha-ha

Pain, sorrow
This is sad
Cry- boohoo

Fear, terror
This is scary
Scream- Agh!

Hope, pray
This is faith
Smile- exhale

Are you going to let them tell you how to act?

Are you going to let them tell you who to become?

You'll be alright kid; we are going to make it.

Purgatory

Alone I sit as I always do
No friends, nobody to keep me company

My heart lurches at the mere thought of it
I catch myself talking to the ghost of an empty room

No one is listening
Traveling upwards, farther away

No one can hear my screams echoing
Help me! Help me before night falls!
Too late
I again sit alone as I always do

Sitting alone as I must

Ruins

Thief! Give me back that of which does not belong to you
What you have stolen is not valuable to anyone
Why did you take it from me?

One slightest twitch of your hand and I am finished
You dare hold it in front of me like a treasure
Without knowing what it could possibly mean?
Had you only asked, I would have given it to you

Thief! Liar! Destroyed by your hand
What you have stolen now crushed by your fingers
Squeezed until it beats no more
I am left to pick up the pieces that lay on the floor

Why did you take it from me?

You never intended to keep it
You never intended to cherish it as I did

Hungry Wolf, Frightened Rabbit

Frightened rabbit, why do you run?
I am nothing more than the big bad wolf

Little frightened rabbit
Don't tire yourself by running
It will do you no good
I will catch you at the end
I always do

Don't run from the big bad wolf
My dearest, frightened rabbit
Your whole life spent
Catapulting yourself away from me

Knowing that in the end
I will catch you as I always do

Deadly III

My lips devour as much as I please
I will take and take and never give

Washing it down with the burning orange afterglow
In the belly of the hog lies the truth

You stand shoving vermin down my throat
Toads surround my tongue

Rodents claw my insides
I will never be satisfied

Nomad

Reaching out with bony fingers
Grasping at a humanity that has abandoned you

A shadow amongst the living
A shell destined to roam but never noticed

What would you give to reach out and touch just one?

You don't belong here, you never did
You never really belonged anywhere, did you?

Faith? Faith has given up on you

Can you hear me now?

Humans, ever seeking a connection
Something to hold on to
A smile in the twilight
A light to shine brightly

You have blinded me
Wounded me so I could not see
Humans in masses
Reaching for one another
Grasping for something
Only caught by a few

Ever searching
A connection!
Sizzle, crack
A spark, then blackness
Slipping through your fingers
Connection lost
Signal gone
Dial tone

Must have been bad reception

A Place

There is a place where lonely people must go
Oh, what a place it is!

Wandering amongst flowers and trees
Singing birds and magnificent sunshine
Never a single raindrop has escaped the sky

What's this?

A group of lonely people arriving spectacular in this place
People coming for solace, basking in the company of each other

Never to be lonely again

Cairdeas

You have illuminated my darkness
Just a quick simple little flash
You came to me just in time
When I feared I might jump and crash

In my hour of need, you were there
Scurrying around me without a care
You looked and found me through this tangled mess
Freeing me of sorrow with just a small caress

As we walk together
Until the bitter end
Please know I love you with all my heart
My sweetest friend

Inevitable

We laugh and play throughout the day
All the while we feel inside
As though we are about to cry

The pain you put inside my chest
Is grim and intolerable at best
You write me off as if I am nothing
While I lay here in silent suffering

No crying, no weeping
Barely any sleeping

Bottled up inside, I think I'd rather die
My organs you've torn and devoured
Onto your next conquest within an hour

Alone I sit, pondering death
About to take my very last breath
Leaving the world as I came in

Naked and alone again

Daisy

Dear little dog how I love you
Sitting here staring at me with big brown eyes
My heart begins to grow twice its size
Through laughter and tears

Through triumph and fears
Throughout all of these years
Please know this is true
Dear little dog how I love you

Always trying to make me feel better
With slobbering kisses wetter and wetter
Without you, I don't know what I would do
Dear little dog how I love you

When the time comes that you must leave us
We will cry and we will fuss
But remember it's because from the start
You left yourself branded on my heart
You brought friendship into my life, an abundance of smiles too

Dearest littlest dog of mine, how I love you

Growth

There is wickedness in you, let me fix it
You have issues child, let me fix you

Understand me, darling, I'm just here to help
Quit moping about, marked with that frown
Your face constantly turned upside down

As if it is some sort of warning label

Hands that reach for you melt away in disdain
Solitude is the fortress you've built
Nothing can touch you, not even the rain

If you are ever lonely just open your door
Reach for hands that reach for you no more

The sun is shining

The birds are singing

I fear you have locked yourself away and you will never know
The warmth you can feel when love helps you grow

Extinguished

You are the reason for the smile on my face
You've fixed the broken
You've put the pieces in their place
Head over heels but can't utter a word
Scared you will see me and take flight
Like a winged bird off into the night
I need you to quench this thirst inside me
To grow and find out what this might be
The desire is building
Clawing up to the surface
One touch I will be a goner
One kiss I will be dust
Burnt by the flame that became us
Don't fizzle out, please no! Not yet
I'd be lost without you, though we just met
Say it isn't so, don't let this be
When you look into the fire, please... remember me

Flight

On this journey by yourself
There will be times you must embark
To the sounds of a lonely lark
Getting lost can be quite scary
The situation becoming hairy
Here again you have been lured
By the cry of the mournful mockingbird

Sometimes the paths you choose are dirty and foul
You must be cautious, be careful
Hoots the ominous owl
Walk ahead with your head held high
I know you seem in a pinch
Once in a while you must walk aside the fearful finch

Temptations are plenty catching your eye
Slipping and tripping us, evil purred
In will fly the regretful redbird
There may be turmoil
This winding road full of dismay
Crying out with the broken blue jay
Falling as your knees hit the ground
Mindful of what is yet to be found
Sit and listen if you will, to hear the story of the worried whippoorwill
My child everything will be alright
When you can take no more and your faith is narrow

Rejoice with me the good and bad
For all the while your guide will be
The beautiful singing sparrow

Liberate

A fire slowly growing inside
As you crawl up my skin
Crashing against me like the rolling tide
Heavy breathing inhale, exhale
Do you feel the beating of my heart?
Do I mean to you, what you mean to me?

Nervous, anxious energy finally free
Rocking with me back and forth
Harder and faster almost there
Explosions of fireworks
Your eyes meeting mine
Together we have crossed that line

The look in your eyes, sorrowful and sad
All at once I know my place
All at once I know the answer

Shame burning my body, charring my skin
Laying amongst the ashes and coal
Where love once lived burning with sin

Deadly IV

Our bodies lay quaking like the earth
Long horns poke and prod at my insides

Nervous energy flowing through the ground
Blue fog suffocates the world around us

Herding me exactly into that place of sin
Sulfur and brimstone tinge my senses

Fire and smoke douse my breath

So Very Tired

Did I even wake up today?
The smell of stale cigarettes and desperation envelop my being
Smoke burns my eyes
Is this my reality?
Muddling day to day
Feeling nothing and everything at once
God I don't want to be here
Take another hit
Down another drink
Pull the blankets to my face
Just let me sleep

Deadly VII

I look on as the rams bleat under the pale blue sky
Lead fills my skull

Weariness leaks from my pores as my bones turn to stone
Thinking overshadowed, languor sinks its teeth in

Serpents close in around my legs
Heaviness lines my body as I droop and dance to an off key tune

Cubicle

Click, type, drool, repeat
BASH MY FACE AGAINST MY DESK
Click, type, drool, repeat

Melancholy

Sorrow running bone deep
A melodic indie song coursing through my veins

The moon beaming down
Powerful stares pierce the night
Flowing from my fingertips I have never felt so alive

A dam within me breaking
Is it trying to free me?
Like a raft tearing down the river towards sanctification

Or is it trying to drown me?
Like a hurricane dragging me under the current

Palpable

Look at me for real
Like I am beautiful
Like I am the only radiance left on a dreary day

Kiss me for real
Like I am the last drop of sunshine left
Like I am the only warmth that will thaw your hypothermic skin

Love me for real
Like I am the oxygen keeping you alive
Like I am your last breath left before you drown

Lie to me for real
Like I might mean anything to you
Like I am the only person you can see

Leave me for real
Like I am a film that has ended
Like I am the rolling credits you didn't care to stick around for

Deadly I

It was I that turned the divine man depraved
Galloping through him like a deranged stallion

It was I that turned the holy man heinous
Screaming as the sun sets into a violet sky

None else holds the power I wield
Laying broken on the ever spinning wheel

Vanity coats my veins
Mirrored glass falls to the floor

Hello My Name is: Self Doubt

I am a dream condemner, quite opposite of a dream crusader
If you wave your flag in my face, I will burn it
If you build your hopes up from nothing, I will demolish them

I am a dream antagonist, quite opposite of a dream apostle
Nothing you want will flourish here
If you show me your heart, I will put heaviness in it
If you look me in the eyes, I will put sadness there

I am a dream crusher, quite opposite of a dream catcher

Legion

WE are blood
WE are sturdy and stocky and tough
WE do not quit

WE are blood
WE are gentle and compassionate and kind
WE care too much

WE are blood
WE are rage and fear and anxiety
WE will rise above

WE are blood
WE are a compass, a leader, and a follower
WE will not let you down

Sinsear

Thousands of women speak to me
Telling me their stories
Telling me their heartaches and joys
Telling me their loves and losses

Thousands of men speak to me
Telling me their trials
Telling me their sorrows and smiles
Telling me their pride and disappointments

Thousands of people led me to this point
I am here because of them
I grow listening to their tales
As they whisper to me in the night

They are flowing through my veins
They give me strength and show me the way
I am but a shaky artist's soul made up of a thousand splintered pieces of my
ancestors

Astéria

The smell of thunderstorm surrounds me
The scent of ozone burns my nostrils
Ionized water clouds my mind as I beg gravity to release me

The atmosphere fills my lungs
I reach for a place I do not know
Longing for a love I have long lost

Craving exploration to find where my soul feels free
The cosmos hold my home I am sure
The celestials cradle the very place I belong

I am ethereal in the presence of Gaia

I am the Goddess of my constellation

Blind Eye

Do you ever stop and ponder?
About the men that wander
From city to city, from town to town
Destined to never truly settle down

Do you ever stop to recognize?
The women with emptiness in their eyes
Images swirling through their brains
Crying over the blood soaked stains

Do you ever stop to examine?
Their sanity dying of famine
Starving for something to make sense
Emotions always straddling a fence

Do you ever stop to reason?
With people that commit treason
Torn between wrong and right
Decisions keeping them up at night

Do you ever stop and brood?
Over the thousands this country has screwed
Defending us in wars they fought in
Arriving home to be forgotten

Oddity

Here I am with my weirdness
My cabinet of curiosities
My box of obscure sorrows

Here I am with my heart on my sleeve
My oddities leaking on your white carpet
My peculiar unfamiliar traditions

Here I am seeking redemption from your judgments
My irregular, abnormal heartbeat sounding in your ears
My sporadic sentences barely understandable

Here I stand with my weirdness
My security strong with the knowledge
My weirdness will never leave me

Night Hawk

Your presence hovers near me
Pecking at my eyes
Pulling at my hair
Trying to get me to remember
Nagging the back of my mind
"Never Forget!"
"Never Forget!"
How will I ever recall anything with you screaming at me?
I lay here trying to get comfortable
My eyes closed, praying sleep will come
But there is only you

Golem

Their faces replaced by telephones
Their insides replaced by computer parts
Motherboards where brains used to be

Advancing faster than ever imagined
Soon they will know everything about you
Soon they will plot and map your life

Every second of every day they will be there
This is the price we must pay to be connected
But hey, look on the bright side. Free Wi-Fi

Deadly II

Rabid thoughts fall from my lips
Madness will soon consume me, haunting the corners of my mind
Bleeding vocal chords continue to scream out

The same phrase repeats over and over again
Like the thundering bark of a hound from hell

Eyes turning green, mouth foaming over
Bone chilling water fills my lungs

My last thought "Why not I?" frozen on my tongue

Early Bird

Skeletal fingers grasp a coffee cup
Warmth coating his throat as he waits to greet the day
He never wakes up

Comfort

I am your safe space
Wistful bookstore on my breath
Hot tea in my veins

Hildr

Screeching, battle cries piercing the night
Choosers of the fallen
Come to offer sanctuary to those that fought so bravely

"I'm sorry" she whispered "I tried"
Sh hush my love, you made us very proud
Strong arms encircling the chosen

Carrying them to a place of beauty and legend
A pair of golden wings shining in the night
Offering a beacon of hope

Onward to Valhalla

Necrosis

I saw the sky blue one last time
Before it off and turned gray
I saw the grass green one last time
Before the colors there did fade

I saw the beauty all around
Before I was put into the ground
I saw the people gather here
Before I sent up one last prayer

I saw your skin pure and fair
Before my last breath from me did tear
I saw your tears like crystals fall
Before Death for me did call

Made in the USA
Middletown, DE
12 February 2019